Tt

Bela Davis

Abdo
THE ALPHABET
Kids

abdopublishing.com

Published by Abdo Kids, a division of ABDO, PO Box 398166, Minneapolis, Minnesota 55439.
Copyright © 2017 by Abdo Consulting Group, Inc. International copyrights reserved in all countries.
No part of this book may be reproduced in any form without written permission from the publisher.

Printed in the United States of America, North Mankato, Minnesota.

102016
012017

THIS BOOK CONTAINS
RECYCLED MATERIALS

Photo Credits: iStock, Shutterstock

Production Contributors: Teddy Borth, Jennie Forsberg, Grace Hansen

Design Contributors: Christina Doffing, Candice Keimig, Dorothy Toth

Publisher's Cataloging in Publication Data

Names: Davis, Bela, author.

Title: Tt / by Bela Davis.

Description: Minneapolis, Minnesota : Abdo Kids, 2017 | Series: The alphabet |
    Includes bibliographical references and index.

Identifiers: LCCN 2016943900 | ISBN 9781680808964 (lib. bdg.) |
    ISBN 9781680796063 (ebook) | ISBN 9781680796735 (Read-to-me ebook)

Subjects: LCSH: English language--Alphabet--Juvenile literature. | Alphabet
    books--Juvenile literature.

Classification: DDC 421/.1--dc23

LC record available at http://lccn.loc.gov/2016943900

Table of Contents

Tt

Talia eats a sweet treat.

Tt

Who is **t**aller, **T**y or **T**iana?

6

Tt

Taylor likes her tire swing.

Tt

Tori sets up a tent.

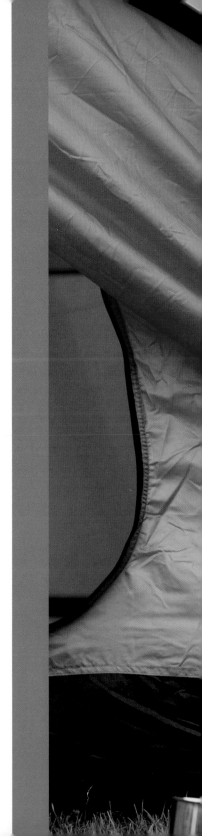

Tt

Tiff **t**ies her **teal** shoes.

Tt

Tessa thinks tulips are pretty.

15

Tt

Ted has a lot of **talent**.

Tt

Tim lost his tooth.

Tt

What does Tom play?

(tennis)

More **Tt** Words

teacher

train

tomato

turtle

Glossary

talent
a special and natural ability to do something well.

teal
a blue-green color.

Index

abdokids.com

Use this code to log on to abdokids.com and access crafts, games, videos, and more!

Abdo Kids Code:
TTK8964